Top 20 New & Innovative Business Ideas

Table of Contents

Introduction

We are living in a world wherever everyone wants to make extra money and add to his income. Most people have achieved this by acquiring great business ideas. When one starts up a company, he must be ready to meet competition. It is important to note that you would not need to become rich or popular to succeed in business but have to think smartly.

The initial point of business is defined when you talk about a product for sale. The knowledge about the definition of business is necessary upright the company to the correct position. A company has to accurately define about their business and it will help for knowing the business ideas. It will also help to know different changes in the environment. This change will help for understanding the advantages and essential things that help to understand what are you struggling for.

The right definition of the business of a company has many advantages. The definition would tell the proper works of the firm that have not been known in any way. The weaknesses would be brought to light by the proper definition of business. A company can highlight its possible faults which have happened before judging that have been taken by a proper definition of the business. Your company's aims and purpose are focused by following the rules of business.

The understanding of business becomes very hard for the fact where the market is changing and new products are taken over by the old ones. When new products come to the market, they will change the current limits which make business rule quite a task. This will not be wrong to say that the business limits are becoming unstable till you are very careful. There are options for getting the loss if a company describes its business as well as signs it.

Chapter 1

Initial knowledge of business

A smart entrepreneur must have a clear knowledge of the particular field he wants to get involved in. He needs to conduct enough on the type of project he intends to start. This knowledge is acquired by reading business articles from magazines, newspapers, and newsletters among other magazines. A different method must be talked with people who are well-known in the business world and any other good source that one can find.

It would be vital that you consider for your income and capital. You should not start up a business project that needs more capital than you can provide. This will help you to get standard profit. So, it goes without saying that the planning of business is very essential. When you fail to plan, you will also fail to get the best profit. As you are an entrepreneur, you have to make a plan on how to start your business.

A wise entrepreneur needs to be able to identify the pick and off pick seasons for his business. It will help in planning and supplying. You need to realize that as an entrepreneur, you are not a boss of your business but a servant. In order to get the fruit in your business, you must be equipped to work hard.

Business networking

Without a strong foundation, a building will not last for many years. Similarly, a business will not last for many times without a strong and wide network. The business networking is one of the best foundations for every successful business.

All company's aim is to be successful with their services and to help from developing powerful networks by creating connections, skill and responsibility. You need to keep in mind that trust is the essential element in creating a strong network for your business.

Business networking is effective and also for low-cost marketing style. You can start this with your friends and coworkers who can take help of your current business relations. First of all, you need to increase your sales opportunities and contacts that are based on appointments and overviews by trying to involve a head on meetings and gatherings. You can use e-mail, phone and raise social and business networking websites to contact. Another thing you need to survey about your neighboring business competitor. Almost, all great number of main businesses has their own associations. Try to connect with these associations for your help of reference as well as a personal introduction if you get that opportunity to start your own networking is hard.

Identify that every professional outside of the business community can be very useful in networking contacts. Usually, think outside the people, you would see at business events on developing networking plans. There are some essential connections that are not for businessmen; so you need to be inspiring to reach them.

The next thing must be learning how to build good business networks and relations. The purpose is when your network is strong to other business they would be more referring to their own circle. Each time make an effort in building just by welcome them as they pass by and make them feel important. The starting is by simple discussion and by telling them that their business is deeply appreciated. By putting your business networks comfortable and striking up, the predictable announcement would help them to know about you. The competitors can be gained by your network and will not be upset.

The value of business communication

Really, the business communication is valuable to you and your professional service company. It is a matter of how well you communicate with your consumers and clients. Your staff needs quality communication; otherwise, you can you depend on their proven abilities.

These can be seemed, like funny questions to ask, but you would be astonished by the similarly funny answers some people give. The business is made on relations and quality relations depend on quality communication. Business communication is the cleanest form that translates right to your bottom line.

In fact, the marketplace is full of any professional service and competition is ferocious. Well, know marketers can realize the exceptional level of opportunity that is available today. In order to survive and prosper in this environment, companies have to know about the oldest method of marketing that won't work anymore. Now, the one-way communication, marketing publicity and company attentive messages are long over. The business communication needs a dialog focused on the needs of the client.

Business communication means reaching out

Definite means, you can use to keep the lines of business communication open with past customers and current prospects. Here are given few tips for staying in touch and inviting dialog.

- You need to send articles that are related to a client's industry. Remove and send the article with a note that is interested in seeing this.
- When their company is said about the better performance of article, use it as a prospect to get in touch. Remove the article, print out the web page and then send a handwritten memo by commending them on the publicity. Send an admiring note to your contact as soon as your company wins an award.

- In your field, search for the possible new areas of action. You've got a reason to make a contact with your client whenever an assembly makes a move in your industry.

Chapter 2

How to start a business?

The starting of a business can be as easy as it takes and is a good planning to strike that start button is operating the business. This is suggested to think about your laying down ideas and future aims for your business. There are some effective businesses stories which are a good practice to put down your plans.

You have some ideas in mind about how to plan for starting a business. This is essential to consider about the risks. This type of risks can bring the full potential of your business. On the other hand, it can be your business alarming. It would never be a problem if you plan for other business ways and plans when anything fails.

For marketing your products and services, you need to use business media. Come up with a place where your consumers generally go. You can consider of using the internet in marketing your products and services. The internet can be your first select for starting a business. The online business advertising can cause the following:

- Lots of progress of your business
- The speedy growth of a number of customers
- Low-cost of product marketing

This is a must to understand that the media can use for increasing and marketing your business and show you are noticeable resolved on why you offer such products and services. You are trying for opening a business that must show the stability when you show your marketability on the internet through the message. The message must be efficient and ranged to what you offer. The starting of a business by the wrong message can lead to its near end. It can be escaped when you take a message which is updated, suitable to the tastes of your customers.

The best time to start a business

People who had great ideas about the common need and fixed to move ahead by opening a storefront and working into business for themselves. We got off that way though serious financial times are producing our American population to start very considering and becoming entrepreneurs again.

There are always blows and dips in the economy though there are products and services which will be required by the general population. You can consider the things that you generally do well. The things you have an honest desire about and then consider raising a business about those talents and interests. Money is considered as one thing but if you do not like what you are doing, the money will not ever come. You are more likely to prosper if you are passionate about your selected profession.

Southwest management determined that it will be more advantageous for them without run out of luxurious airport hubs where they would have entered air carriers. Therefore, the lesson here is to search for the business signs which are watching you in the face and then progress a business plan. This plan will let you take full benefit of the current business condition.

You can know that your personal abilities are very well as a small business owner, you will have to know to keep your new company running adeptly. The problem finding by customers comes up to your company and takes an attempt to overcome it. Moreover, you will need to know about sales, marketing, business growth, accounting and how this new plan will affect your own economic life. There are not many of us who can do, all of these works well and so you need to hire somebody to do some of these things for you. Get an accountant to handle your banking, accounting, and tax matters. Try to become educated in some of the other issues at your limited community college at the local book shop. On the internet, there would be a class about specific topics that offered online via webinar or on CD.

The best business to start with no original costs

One of the best businesses to start will be the low startup charges. It is essential to acquire a bank loan to start a business. You need lots of capital upfront to finance your creativity if you want to open a shop. For this, you need money to rent a place, money to buy shop and money to pay for marketing. Those are considering three cases out of many costs causes.

Now, on account of the internet, the nature of business has improved and it is no longer required to have physical properties. You have an effective shop and still sell the same things. It is possible to sell lots of material because you have limited floor space in a rented shop.

This can reach a much larger customer base. Ideally, you can reach anybody who has a connection to the internet throughout the world. The nature of shopping has fully changed by the Web and so the best business will be one that takes help of the medium. The people are less expected to go to the mall to buy clothes or the local shop to buy food. The whole thing can be done by online.

The fully working business can be set up in the online for little or no money. That has seemed as the real beauty and no one can omit it. You do not need to be well fit to get good credit rating which is a lengthy business plan. The aim is that you should not sit before manager for loans at your local bank. There you have no need to try and verify that your dream is going to be achieved. You just make a start and get happening.

There is something that is based on online, is the best business to start. You have almost no costs and it is much easier to test and see what you work for. There might not be anything worse than investing thousands into opening elements. The mortar business is only to see for the high operating costs and low limits.

Opening something on the Internet means your overheads are extremely low and you can get benefit from a much larger produce margin. You do not need to pass the following thirty years that responding away for some big company in an office. You can realize the best business to start if you want something else. This method is the life that you want to start a business and you can get three plans for businesses.

The best small business to start

There are many methods; you can start a small business online with very small capital. Here describe 4 main means to earn money online. These methods are multi-level marketing, affiliate and internet marketing, foreign exchange and playing poker.

- **Foreign exchange:** There are many people who are earning their living from online by using Foreign Exchange. These systems are sale which you want to buy. The important fact to success is to stick the system and having a lot of correction. There is a danger that the system will work contrary to you. If you learn how to be ordered enough and are capable of taking the irregular loss of capital and this is the best small business to start.

- **Affiliate and internet marketing:** This is the best small business to start that is popular to all. Affiliate and internet marketing is the way, you can make money free online, deprived of risking any security. On the other side of the range, if you have lots of money, you can make vast internet marketing. If you select to start an affiliate or internet marketing business, the only thing you need to invest your education.

- **Multi-level marketing:** Multi-level Marketing can be the business for you if you feel like a publics' figure and you have a strong partiality to motivate people to success. Many people have this shame about multi-level marketing. You can think about this way and there is no way you can lose. You can get training that is given to a course, must cost you ten to thousands of dollars. It is certainly something to think about. It can be the best small business for you to start.

- **Playing poker online:** The top poker players are used to make millions of dollars in a year. This is made like a system that impacted to it and having 100% belief in it. They get the special bad hits and they always trust that if they stick to the system, they will finish up earning a profit. If you have the ability for pleasure, most of the time playing poker online is the best small business for you to start.

Chapter 3

Business Opportunities

The idea of a business opportunity must not be wholly understood as it can apply to many different conditions. Here, we will not be speaking about license opportunities. Almost, everything goes from supplier to sell machine ways, starting from network advertising to dealers. The business opportunities can be online or can be placed in the actual world. A business opportunity is the sale or rent of a product, service or tools which allow you to start a business.

Usually, business opportunities include a product and they have a position through the online world is rapidly moving. The theory of the business opportunity is that there is a fixed bazaar for selling the product. The original fees for taking benefit of a business opportunity can differ and there can be a promising facility. Usually, business opportunities accompany some kind of marketing program too.

Generally, a business opportunity does not mention to the unique sale of a free business. The business opportunities contain a method that can be sold to more than one buyer in one location. There are generally no duties between the seller and the buyer with the sale of a free business. Buyer can do everything according to their want with the business they have accepted, and there is no necessity for a current relationship with the seller.

There are a lot of rewards and benefits connected with business opportunities. Usually, they have a lower fee and lower startup prices which are permeable. Business opportunities are built on a verified method, so you can yield from the skill of others. Here contain a training program that is connected with the business opportunity and wide term of business can be available too. Your advantage from the buying rule of a bigger company and you can take help of the supportive progressive activities and marketing.

The world business opportunities are not perfect all the time. The company is advising the opportunity that cannot have the best benefits in mind. There can be a lack of care at some times. Exceptionality, parts can delay your ability to compete in the market. This is not useless for parent companies. Anytime you can get a return by taking benefit of a new business opportunity and it is your duty to assess both the company and yourself.

Besides, having the economic freedom to take a chance, you have the desire and interest to give a new business opportunity. You have enough time easily to take the success of this business opportunity.

The starting up new business needs full knowledge of your product or else service. You must move away from this certain opportunity if the company is not willing to offer that knowledge. You have to study the company's record of past success and search for interview somebody who is now involved with the business opportunity.

You must look for promises of practical profits; all at once there must be no limit on future income. Promises of the fast and easy resources must be an advice for you to stay away. There is no lack of business opportunities available. This is a simple matter to find that appeal to your interests and fits in your startup budget. Don't let yourself be rushed into any plan. Correct business opportunities based on sure models will have no worry waiting for your careful attention.

International business opportunity

The using of the popular search engines when a new entrepreneur considers by offering into an international business opportunity and chooses to research the available opportunities is very small information to be originated. It is clear that there are hundreds to thousands of persons involved in the business opportunity. But, definitely, the common limit is to consider more traditional opportunities. If not fascinating to the search, an international business opportunity and more accurately a general network marketing international business opportunity.

Let's take a examine to the cultural and technical growths which have come about in the past 15 to 20 years that make it possible, and perhaps desirable before learning into international business opportunity. Great steps in communications knowledge brought about a great amount by the progress and solar growth of the internet have made rapid public services with a view, customer or business assistant in the simple and very cheap way. The start of email and video conferencing has made it as easier as to contact with the people who is situating at a long distance.

Because of these trends in technology, it is likely to combine the 'business opportunity', the 'home business opportunity' and the "network marketing business opportunity" into one exciting worldwide business that is the end of a home office with a computer. There are a small number of leading edge companies that are working this way with all of the tools of nationally or internationally to be wholly correct.

Sometimes, the secondary sales mentioned to as back-end sales can be products, services or devices that are essential and important part of the operation of the business and to improve the income made by the business. It is possible that a little profitable situation can be achieved by the secondary sales.

The primary business is considered as an essential part of the international business opportunity and it must be selected with great care. There are a number of features that must be thought carefully. These include:

- The company needs unique products which will serve many different market and demand to the crowds.
- Company management must have been effective business leaders and have a dream for future development.
- The company must be firm, must have been in business for at least 15 to 20 years and have the capability to make long-term sales.
- Definite systems have to follow the company which is simple and duplicable for product marketing as well as supply.
- It must return totally and have an aim of making a control in the world.
- It has to payout at best 50% of sales, offer infinite depth within the reward plan and must offer important fast start bonuses.

Business loan strategies

Borrowers must understand that business loan choices will be meaningfully different when related to a business buying that can be learned with a commercial property loan. This difficult condition happens for the lack of commercial real estate because security for the business financing when buying a business opportunity. Efforts to buy a business opportunity are that always defined by commercial drops as really confusing and difficult for arranging the business loan.

There are comments and proposals in this report to duplicate business financing situations which are generally offered by large banks, eager to offer a business loan to buy a business opportunity. For these conditions, in which a seller will secretly fund the gaining of a business opportunity and it is not our intent to address that business loan promises in this report.

- **Buying a business opportunity:** The business backup conditions are to buy a business opportunity, will often contain a reduced profit age compared to profitable loan financing. The full term of ten years is usual, as well as the business loan is possible to want a commercial contract capable of the length of the loan.

- Down payment expectations to buy a business opportunity: A usual down payment for business supporting to buy a business opportunity is 20 to 25 percent liable for the kind of business. There are some financing from that the seller will be seen as useful by a commercial lender. Then seller financing must fall the business opportunity down for fee necessity.

- **Probable interest rate costs for buying a business opportunity:** The type to buy a business opportunity is about 11 to 12 percent in the present profitable loan. A practical level of business opportunity is by copying because it is not rare for a commercial real estate loan. For the lack of commercial stuff, security in a small business opportunity deal, the cost of a business loan to get a business that is regularly higher than the rate for a commercial property loan.

- **Buying a business opportunity:** The selection of a commercial lender is to be an essential part of the business which is in the financing method. So the main job is escaping lenders who are unable to confirm a commercial loan for buying a business. By removing such problem lenders, the business borrowers will be in a good position to avoid many new business loan problems. The active method is to avoid problem and owners can have double aids as it will pay for the long-term financial condition of the business and the final success of the commercial loan.

- **Refinancing choices when buying a business opportunity:** A serious commercial loan term to suppose when gaining a business opportunity that is refinancing business opportunity. Presently, there are a few business financing programs being advanced which are likely to advance future business refinancing choices. An acute importance of it is to place the best terms when buying the business and not depend upon business opportunity refinancing possibilities.

Chapter 4

Innovative ideas to start a business

Most of the time, people wish that they might be a boss of their own business and make their personal hours and live a life according to their own choice. This idea can be a truth for an owner of a small business. There is a large cost in owning your own business which starts with thinking an innovative and limited idea. You would turn over what makes you happy and calculate how you would love to spend your time when thinking about your small business idea. These contacts are related as soon as we think about childhood and we enjoy spending our free period.

You can associate two of your interest's intro one business idea like your love of music and children that are seeing an idea for a music studio for children. Write any other business ideas which contain your interests and those do not seem probable.

Consider the truth of starting a business in your life by bearing in mind about money and other limitations. Then you can remove most of the ideas on your list, wherever ideas will be limited down to one or two true business ideas.

I mean in the next hour and try what I did if you need money. Now I am making more money from my old business, read the fantastic and true story. As soon as I joined, I was doubtful for ten seconds, once I understood what this was. Then I was smiling from ear to ear and you will do it too. Visualize copying your money all week with no or little risk to learn a confirmed list of Million Dollar Corporations by offering you their products at 75% commission.

Some innovative business ideas of the world

With an active original mind, you have so many ideas, in a short amount of time that they cannot write them. This is fewer acts on them to the innovation by starting a business, else hiring a lawyer to help them. I speak from knowledge when I say that if you are not going to feast on your creations and innovations, then those ideas to some company that would be able to use those concepts.

All over in the world arose with good enterprise ideas and also coming from the entrepreneur himself, his creative team and some of his family members. The good enterprise ideas are around the corner and it takes a business-minded person to allow them. Sometimes good business ideas have started to most profitable businesses. However, the people behind the enterprise did not stop with just having the enterprise ideas. There can be various difficult works that stem from good business ideas with planning, the progress of the enterprise and marketing movement.

There are some people who give you good business ideas by motivation. This looks because they risked on their enterprise ideas as a problem of luck with no difficult work. Most people have acquired book and journal available, visited many enterprise races and thought with as many persons as possible to offer you good enterprise thoughts.

The person who is very creative and has many saved information can create the best business ideas. Generally, some people join trade shows and business meetings and seminars to provide you with good enterprise ideas and to improve the ideas they have. By joining trade events and shows, you could be a person who is examining for enterprise ideas. The current businesses that are on the exhibition can provide you a thought of what kind of business goes. He can offer you with innovations of current businesses. Usually, most of the entrepreneurs who have learned good business ideas assume out of the box. It means they will not limit themselves to what's already there. They think creative and at times they assume silly. Some businessman thinks about the times that persons make as a reason to spend like Valentines, Christmas, Easter, birthdays, and Halloween. There are some people who continue from finding their business area.

The people who know the tips on how to cook can arise with a house business through certain occasions. He can take order for a heart made sweets and design the creation with a modified touch. There is another good business idea like flower delivery. All enterprise ideas can be achieved without the need for investing lots of capital for rentals. Lots of good business ideas that have not ever been appointed. Some have been tried and observed and they could have failed for lack of some materials.

Chapter 5

Home based business idea

A different home based business idea that is remaining about in your head and you are eager to get partially. It is the best time to join that energy and make the business you have been seeing about. The beginning of a business is simple if you know the basics. When you know what you need to do for a business and then you can make the business of your dreams.

Firstly, you must consider when you get that new home based business idea. If people are going to buy your item or service, you can take a close search about the market for your new home based business idea. You have a narrow idea to definite topics when you find that your new home based business idea is not new. You should find the area which needs what you have to deal the most and the correct area for your new home based business idea.

Then check the laws in your state. You need to make confirm that you have the correct licenses and guarantee to offer your product or service, depending on your new home based business idea. You need to state for coming out and ensure a check if you are opening a day care center from your home. Then you need to complete special paperwork. You are required to get a business license for your new home based business idea. The procedure with your town to see what is necessary. The business license is cheap.

A new good idea is to make a business plan for your new home based business idea. A business plan lets you make aims and values of your new home based business idea. You can find suitable in the future. It lets you see how you want to run your business. It does not take long to write a business plan and it is generally one of the most valuable tools for making your new home based business idea.

You will be taking some time to measure your economic needs because you are making your business plan for your new home based business idea. Then, you need to fix your operating charges. If you need to get a business loan to get your new home based business idea up and running. You will certainly need a business plan when you apply for loans or search for depositors. What your new home based business plan will need, you should take a look in the long and short term to choose.

Marketing means placing yourself out of there and marketing your business all the time. For this, you need to join networking groups and give off flyers. You can place ads in newspapers and magazines if it is sensible. You do not need to do all at the same time, but always keep your eye on increasing your new home based business idea.

- **Part time home based business idea**: First decision is to start with your home based business idea by way of a part time job. Many entrepreneurs take this method. This method supports you in modifying the threat which is usually related to starting a new business. However, you have your job if your home based business idea fails. You can take it up such as a full-time business when you have your home based business idea doing well. The key problem with working a home based business idea as a part time business is preserving the stability between your part time home based business idea and your full-time job. You must turn out by messing up if you do not plan really well. Running your home based business idea in extra time will mean that you do not have more time for your family. Maintaining the attention on two things is not an easy job. The development of your home based business idea will be slower than what it might be.
- **Full-time home-based business idea:** You would leave your full-time job and start faithfully with your home based business idea if you plan to take the fall straight away. You need to be assured of the success of your home based business idea in such a case. You would have examined your home based business idea enough in order to provide you the assurance of going all out. You must have a backup plan if the home based business idea does not deliver according to your prospects. Do not show all your savings into your home based business idea; save some amount to shelter your living costs too. The running of your home based business idea is equally a full-time job will help you in maintaining a better balance between work and

family. You would be capable of planning and implement better and later see your business rise quicker with more time on hand.

Chapter 6

Top 20 list of business ideas

You can ask this essential question about how to start a business. This is a good time for starting up a business by the help of the economy. I find no matter about the economy and it is easier to start a business than finding the exact job. There is a trick for me to find an amazing, low-cost but useful business to start. I have good business ideas for you and that will always avoid end windows. You will not ever end to these people who would love to pay for doing the work.

This business is great as you can make fast income when you start. It will be surprised to you for investing a small amount of money and gaining more profit. Operating charges is negligible related to the amount of money which you will give to your pocket. You will get paid at the end of all jobs.

This would be the ticket for you that you are searching for the exact job. Window washing business is not ever dull since there is plenty of learning about the industry. You will always make consultation with new people and then every day act in itself. At that time, you will get to move from place to place and work indoors and outdoors.

An additional benefit to owning your own window coating business is that you can do this full-time, part-time job for extra income. You will really become your own boss if you work full-time, control of your own costly time by planning for the most of the clients. You can choose the days; you leave rather than the other way and take control of your own future on behalf of somebody telling you.

There are given below top 20 new and innovative business ideas:

1. **Event planning:** There are fewer parents who have the time to fix and establish their kid's birthday party. When you are a woman with abilities to

combine a meeting and get work done from your workers and becoming an event planner must be the best business idea for you. The event planning still being a necessary business, women with their natural ability for uniting and getting things done, can certainly make their mark in the business.

2. **Grocery shopping:** The lengthy rows and people flood in the grocery shop and have made grocery shopping as a pain in these days. People have started defining ways of having their groceries that sent to them at their doorways. This business model has showed the report more accurate and leads Instacart that is making all month. A grocery supply service can be one kind of small business ideas for women.

3. **Masseuse:** Sometimes, a massage facility at their home is somewhat that any person would desire for. A massage service business would make the essential income with a small outlay for marketing your service in the locality. Through the appeal for demand services on the rise, massage service is an extra choice for women to start a business.

4. **Offline consulting:** Internet marketing demand and SEO skills is all time high and local mothers' pop small business owners and are ready to pay four figures for or simple SEO jobs.

5. **PPC:** The Pay Per Click marketing is far from being new. On the other hand, it is still one of the easiest methods for small business owners and also internet marketers to earn economic success. If you are supporting affiliate offers services, PPC can bring in new leads.

6. **Mail Order:** About fully thought over the last decade, direct marketing by using 'snail mail' is the method of letters and is making new lucky because the fight has fallen boldly in the internet and email marketing.

7. **Sell advertising space on your blog:** If you have a blog or a website, you can increase an extra income by selling advertising space on it. Many online advertising networks can apply to show their ads that made on your website when this weekend. The most renowned advertising network is Google AdSense. As soon as you have applied and your website is approved, you will get a code that you have to paste on your site to get appropriate content ads featured. When a visitor clicks on the advertisements, you will make money.

8. **Sell crafts online:** This is one kind of weekend business for you if you are creative. The handcrafts such as home-made jewelry; candles, soaps are a

good and quite a cheap way to begin a new weekend business which does not influence in your life. A lot of people have started a business by selling jewelry through online like eBay. Besides, you can get the knowledge to your home-made crafts by earning an income from the side. Some success stories of people have started a crafts business on the weekend which soon bloomed into an effective business.

9. **Affiliate marketing:** This involves supporting the products online in chat for a percentage of the sale. There are lots of big organizations that are ready to write large cheese for people who are successful in sponsoring their products. When there are products you have purchased from online and can speak for their quality, you can earn a profitable income. Here is an opportunity for you to earn money when people click on your links and make a buying.

10. **Become an article writer:** If you are a good write, there are many online writing chances for you to start. Some websites offer online writing jobs that you can apply for and get started for making some money. You can write online by articles or a series of articles on a related subject. You can write sales letters, forum postings, and press releases if you have advertising experience. Some sites in which you can find writing changes in Elance.com, Upwork.com, and Freelancer.com that are looking for bloggers to write blog posts.

11. **CPA:** CPA is commonly known as Cost Per Action that offers where they can make money just by advising consumers to complete an offer without any charge. CPA money making method have exactly increased in the last three years and has become one of the most popular small business ideas. By covering almost every niche thinkable, CPA offer is making millionaires beyond normal affiliate marketers.

12. **Network Marketing:** Network marketing is also commonly known as Multi-Level Marketing or MLM. It has grown throughout the intent marketing trend. There is no longer the 'problem of your family and colleagues' sorts of shoulder to shoulder business model. Now a day, MLM has contained new marketing plans with a passion.

13. **Site Flipping:** Site flipping has earned more fame in the last couple years such as a viable method to make a full-time income from home. There are many web designers who will just crank out an inspiring and looking

website in a certain niche and sell it for a fast $200. Another people will develop a website till it is receiving traffic, and generating income.

14. **PPV:** PPV or pay per view is quite a new traffic generation model wherever marketers can correct steal traffic used for other websites. It is actual controversial and many marketers are trying to work at PPV. This is perfect for list building as well as free CPA offers; PPV deals a chance for low-cost traffic and often time vast profits.

15. **Online Services:** You should not make a link wheel yourself then just hire someone. There are many IM forums that have a service area to catch skilled SEO, web service, article writing as well as any service. So forth skills, you have sold for some fast money.

16. **Web Services:** The creation of internet marketing has laid new opportunity in the service division. When it is SEO, web design, email marketing, back linking or web services will just last to increase in the request.

17. **Warrior Special Offers:** This is also known as WSO's or Warrior Special Offers that are money making systems and is one of the largest marketing forums in the world. Really, there are people who have not anything to do but sell money by making info to members.

18. **Click Bank:** You can have a correct option of affiliates promoting your product by making your own information products and yield them to ClickBank.com. Here all the commission costs are handled by Click Bank themselves.

19. **JV's:** Joint Ventures will remain one of the fastest ways to economic freedom, and in most of the cases total wealth. By joining with the correctly recognized marketers can make all the change in the world.

20. **Article marketing:** Some online sites like AssociatedContent.com will really buy your articles. Besides, the article can be written to help your own product, CPA offer for future commissions.

Chapter 7

Business ideas for women

Many women have a tendency to think that it is difficult to make money online and you have a computer genius to be able to take benefit of the internet. But, the problem is that most of the women have no idea where to start and what areas to turn on.

By using the internet, everybody has the chance to make money and it is all about interest and determination. There are some people who will try hard for a few months and then leave as they are not seeing any effects. The trick is that you love to do and to stick with it by enjoying and make money altogether. Here you have to think about a niche which you can turn on and make your presence online.

You need to think about the things to find your own niche that you are passionate about. Essentially, this is the first step to start your own home based business because you will need to find your desire. The first step is to love what you are doing if you are selling products, blogging, or opening your own business.

There are over 50 women who are aged and thus they want to start their own business. You need to think about the amount of free time when you have to offer even out home based business ideas for women. It is an ideal niche that would allow you to actually focus on developing a successful online business.

- **Become a blogging:** There is lots of money to be made just by starting up a blog. When you are a mother, then you can start a parenting-themed blog wherever you can provide parenting advice to other parents. You will be really taken in a field like this as a woman. You can be pulling an income by either offering advertising on your blog with a cunning name and an exciting angle.
- **Become a virtual assistant:** A good business idea is to become a virtual assistant by working for somebody online, doing the jobs that they are not capable of doing. You can think of it because being an assistant to somebody rather than having to go into the office. If you are capable of finding the

exact employer, this can be the best one among many business ideas for women.

- **Sell information:** When you have something which you know lots, you can sell that information online. You can make an e-book based on about a subject that interests you and then you will see how a little marketing can help you to sell your informational products. There are a lot of profitable business ideas for women which you can start now. It takes is some resolution and you will be employed for the relief of your own home.

Chapter 8

Innovative information technology ideas

The information technology expert can contract with the modern technology to your task and update your business. These can help you finding the fast and future goals and work in combination with you. Your staff can find the most actual path to their activities.

Your aims will need an updated database management system and the related software that works to store and save your daily, monthly and yearly records. You need to increase your marketing system and consumer conformity systems and bring them nearer to the benefits of computer commands. All of these tasks can be a factor in determining the asset to make in the latest technology.

You can find that new development to computers, networks, and also software that have rushed themselves into well pricing deals and have led many companies to cost savings. A smarter stock chain organization system has appeared that has cut harms of items and better delivery times. These all has added to the lucky position of improving your information processing jobs.

As soon as you spend time with talking what your current system is doing and what extra jobs you want to do, your advisor will find several ways that these ideas can be spoken. These thoughts will be familiar and presented to you for more comment. Definite aims will be decided on your newly updated system and will be in the task.

There is some important demand for an engineer that specifies in virtualization, calculating, cyber safety, software programming, application experts, and technology bosses. Now, we are going to deliver three main causes on why you must choose a career in IT:

- **Innovation:** All the time, IT field is changing and there is new knowledge that is being introduced and old knowledge is being developed. You will have the chance to take part in the job that is changing the way of work and lives. A lot of innovations with the introduction of social networking have permitted people to cooperate and connect from everywhere at all time. The capability to take the news at the moment that occurs for reforming the time and it takes to get evidence. The division among nations and position is becoming irrelevant with the development of video and internet service. Now, companies have the ability to call a meeting over the internet with agents from all over the world joining the meeting. The staff is call up their company data over mobile plans. Companies are now taking benefit of cloud calculating and moving their data from their business assembly.

- **Role of IT in business:** The companies influence of IT to support the formation of new services and to improve their business competence. Now, IT is becoming an important factor for businesses to build good benefit against other companies. IT is used by these companies to distinguish their services and products and to improve more value to their consumers. The need for IT experts and to maintain operations will be a continuous driver of stability for the IT department.

- **Diversity in the profession:** Many different jobs can remain in the IT department that the list of situations is increasing because technology is making new positions. Many different sellers offer their products to support business developments that an IT expert can learn and become involved in. The companies like Oracle, Microsoft, and Cisco that offer seller specific solutions to make opportunities for professionals to learn their software. These sellers provide programs for information labors to use a technical certification which proves their skill to work with their products.

Chapter 9

New and creative business ideas

You do not need to be brilliant to arise with a business idea. This is actually simple to arise with business ideas. Though, the test lies in pending with a business idea which works for you and suits your character as well as necessities.

Most of the people pack up here and many people want to start their own and think about it all the time. It is not a small question that the type of business you are going to start will order if you will be profitable or not.

If you have some kind of outline to get your mind absorbed in business ideas which will get up you and work with your personal condition. You have taken a big step to becoming successful in business.

When you are very busy with your everyday works and return on what you want, but your brain is too worried and lacking the capability to run wild with your mind. Here is given some tips and advice which will help you to start with the creative process.

The first step is to think creatively by understating how the mind works and how to motivate your brain. The brain is consisting of two main parts and these are the right and the left hemispheres. Each of these has not the same functions and works another way. The right hemisphere is the artistic and creative part and it is the part that gains art, colors, and dreams to examine and process information. This is one kind of part that controls creativity and the mind.

The left part is known as the logical part. This is one kind of part that does mathematical calculations, looks for causes and effects. It is also the part which controls speech, word order and grammar.

You need to have a balance on both sides for to run a successful business. You have to be artistic and creative to arise with business ideas and to come about with creative solutions on behalf of business problems. You have to perform logical investigate and describe business opportunities, calculate business threats and consider your options to deal with the daily business matters.

The brain is like a muscle and so if you do not exercise it will not become a shape. You can't fix a lengthy plan by sitting on the sofa every day. The common fences to creative thinking are habits, approaches, everyday routines, lack of assurance for guidance from others. The best method to break those barriers is to be opening minded, be interested in new things, or by just giving your brain the green light to think creatively. Therefore, take the time to think and grow your brain refreshed.

You must change is one of the best methods to stimulate your brain and learn new ideas. The change of scenery will help you to clear your mind on daily issues and provide you some simplicity to start thinking creatively. You can go to a garden, or where you like and take the time to use your brain. The change of people will help you to meet new people and pin your ears back to them talking about their topics. You can gain a good idea and aims that is the source of any successful business. The change of place will certainly help you to discover new ideas that you have not seen or heard earlier. You must see a new kind of store in your journey to Tokyo which you think will work well.

Chapter 10

Most profitable business ideas

Everyone wants to make more money. You must offer some valuable product or services to make money. The cost of any product or services is definite by a buyer. Buyer has many kinds of needs and he looks for the product that is appropriate to his needs. About thousands of people are providing similar kinds of product or services.

There are certain products that are sold on the basis of brand and feature when other are sold on the basis of visual beauty, charm, and extra features. By joining these qualities, you can make a product most profitable and earn a lot of money. You should make a list of the items that are sold on the root of visual beauty and charm to find such sorts of products.

Some of the products can become most profitable that are evidence products. Most of the people are hungry for new and valuable information. Though they cannot buy books, they can buy answers to their problems. When you can please their hunger, this can be a most profitable business for you. This type of products can even bring over 5000% profits.

Moreover, you can sell info products on the internet wherever a one-time asset is essential. You can sell thousands of copies when your info product becomes more popular. You must familiarize something exclusive to make all most profitable. These simple combinations have made many billionaires and also made their own business opportunities and revolved these opportunities into profitable businesses.

Conclusion

Thank you again for downloading this book!

I hope this book was able to help you to understand business knowledge and how can you apply this knowledge in the business field to earn more profit.

To the end, if you enjoyed this book, please take the time to share your thoughts and post a review. It'd be greatly respected!

Thank you and good luck!